Seeing Yourself Through God's Eyes

A Devotional Guide
June Hunt

HOPE FOR THE HEART
P.O. Box 7 • Dallas, TX • 75221
www.hopefortheheart.org

Hope For The Heart is a worldwide ministry with the two-fold mission of providing Bible-based counsel to renew minds, heal hearts, and bring hope to the hurting, while empowering Christians to disciple others.

Seeing Yourself Through God's Eyes

Copyright© 1989, 1999, 2004 by June Hunt

This title is also available as a four-tape or CD Series.
Visit www.hopefortheheart.org

Hunt, June.
　　Seeing yourself through God's eyes / June Hunt.
　　　　p.　　　　cm.
　　ISBN 0-9711792-4-7
　　1. Consolation.　2. Suffering—Religious aspects—Christianity.
3. Devotional calendars　　　　I. Title
BV4909.H76　　　　1989
242'.4—dc20　　　　　　　　　　　　　　　　　　　　89-29187
　　　　　　　　　　　　　　　　　　　　　　　　　　　　CIP

Cover design by Sylvain Mallette

Printed in the United States of America

99 00 01 02 / DC / 22 21 20 19 18 17 16 15 14 13

Dedication

$\mathcal{S}$ometimes we are able to see glimpses of God in the lives of those around us. This book is dedicated to my first "forever friends," who for many years have been the expressions of the love and grace of God to me.

To Barbara Spruill—my "grace friend"
You have given me grace, upon grace, upon grace. I first learned—really learned—the grace of God through you. I see the mercy and grace of God in you.

To Eleanor Briley—my "ethics friend"
Through your life you made me want to live with the highest ethics. I see the love and faithfulness of God in you.

O God, how I thank You for giving me
faithful friends who are extensions of
Your faithfulness and love,
Your mercy and grace.

"Find rest, O my soul, in God alone;
my hope comes from him.
He alone is my rock and my salvation;
he is my fortress, I will not be shaken."
(Psalm 62:5-6)

Contents

Introduction

Seeing Yourself Through God's Eyes

My Position in Christ

His Plan for Me

My Possessions in Christ

His Purpose for Me

Appendices

Introduction

"I pray that out of his glorious riches he may strengthen you with power through his Spirit in your inner being, so that Christ may dwell in your hearts through faith. And I pray that you, being rooted and established in love, may have power, together with all the saints, to grasp how wide and long and high and deep is the love of Christ."
(Ephesians 3:16-18)

Introduction

Dear Friend,

Do you ever feel as though you're on an emotional seesaw—sometimes up—sometimes down? You get a pat on the back . . . you feel really good. You get a stab in the back . . . you feel like a failure! It's as though one end of the seesaw pushes you up because God has given you worth, while the other end plummets you down with the weight of another failure.

Sometimes it's difficult to grasp God's perspective! You may be so crushed by your circumstances that you can't see yourself as God truly sees you. Or maybe you simply don't know how God views you. These 31 daily devotionals will help you see your worth and will remind you that as a believer *you are very special* in the heart and mind of God.

But what if you are emotionally battling with feelings of unworthiness? Perhaps you are the victim of a cruel vengeance . . . you are emotionally battered to the point that you're broken with pain and your heart has lost all hope. Is it possible to accept the truth that you have precious worth?

It might help if you ask yourself, *How is the worth of something established?* Let's assume that you are attending an auction. Time after time the auctioneer sells the items to the highest bidder, whoever was willing to pay the most. Consider this—Christ paid the ultimate price for you when He came to earth as a man, willingly died on the cross and paid the penalty for your sins. Jesus Christ as God did not have to redeem you. But He loves you so much—you are so valuable to Him—that He willingly paid the highest price. Without a doubt, you *have* great worth in His eyes!

By meditating daily for one month on the following Scriptures, you will see your worth and will slide off that emotional seesaw. As you train your mind to focus on the truth about yourself, your emotions will *"be transformed by the renewing of your mind"* (Romans 12:2).

Commit in your heart to faithfully doing these spiritual exercises, taking time to soak up all their truths. Then these Scriptures will begin to saturate your heart, transform your thinking and help to develop the true picture of who you are . . . from God's point of view.

I want this to be an encouraging study for you! My prayer is that because of devoting some time to meet with God, you will take to heart His precious perspective of you. Your emotions will be steadied, your heart will be secured . . . because you will have learned to *see yourself through God's eyes.*

Prayerfully,

June Hunt

What is Your Identity?

Every person born into this world has had difficulty with identity at some time or another. All of us have struggled with our self-image. Many people spend a lifetime manipulating acceptance and attention from others, thinking that they are building an indestructible tower of self-worth. Yet brick by brick, others fail us, and expectations falter. Meanwhile, they miss the vision God truly has of them and the immense value He places on them. However, the steps to understanding these truths are paved throughout Scripture. To tread these steps, we need to have a knowledge of what is meant by IDENTITY.

Have you ever asked, *Who am I? Where am I going?* Do you feel you have little purpose or worth? How essential it is for you to arrive at an accurate conclusion to these questions in order to experience the fullest meaning and purpose for your life!

Realize that your IDENTITY ultimately determines your *worth* and your destination. In a very practical sense, if I were to enter a bank, step up to a teller and say, "May I have $100?" the teller would ask for my name and account number. If I could not provide this information and I continued to request money, I would receive nothing but directions to the front door! However, knowing there are resources in my name, regardless of who placed them there, as long as I provide the teller with my name and account number, I can quickly receive the cash requested. *My identity* definitely determines *my worth* and my ability to draw upon that reserve.

Where am I going? How can you answer this question? Some time ago I was flying from Atlanta to Dallas. I arrived at the airport with time to spare before the final boarding call. I made a quick phone call to my mom, using the extra time I thought I had. When I began to board, I was told they had started assigning seats for standby passengers and that I was to check in at the main desk. There was the possibility my seat may have been given to someone else! My heart raced as I approached the agent at the desk and handed him my ticket. Would I be allowed to get home? A silent eternity passed as he scanned a computer screen for the official flight passenger list. He checked for my name, saw it and said with a smile, "Yes, you are on this flight. You may board the plane." You see, *my identity* was directly linked to the *destination* of that plane.

Much more critical is our identity in terms of *ultimate* worth and *eternal* destination. There are two different "identities" or "families" for all human beings. There are those who are *in Adam* and those who are *in Christ*. *"For since death came through a man, the resurrection of the dead comes also through a man. For as in Adam all die, so in Christ all will be made alive"* (1 Corinthians 15:21-22). The question is: *to which of these two families do you belong?* Your personal identification with one of these families will determine your characteristics and your inheritance.

Our physiological characteristics are determined by our biological families. When I was a freshman in college, my roommate was Josephine Eng from Hong Kong. She had straight black hair, dark brown eyes, a dark complexion, flattened features and a small frame. I had curly blond hair, green eyes, fair complexion, angular features and a large frame. As much as I appreciated Josephine, I could never possess her characteristics. Simply put, I couldn't have Eng characteristics unless I had been born into the Eng family. Likewise, when we were born into the "Adam" family, we inherited characteristics from his family line.

Since Adam made the choice in the Garden of Eden not to obey God, he and all his descendants are identified with sin. This heart of independence is the basic nature that we have all inherited. Psalm 51:5 says, *"Surely I was sinful at birth, sinful from the time my mother conceived me."* Consequently, our natural inclination is to sin because we are born into Adam's family.

However, since God made it possible for us to change families, we are enabled to have a new identity . . . a new nature! You can be adopted into the family of Christ and become "a child of God." You lose your identity in Adam and receive your identity in Christ. You now have new characteristics. *"Therefore, if anyone is in Christ, he is a new creation; the old has gone, the new has come!"* (2 Corinthians 5:17). Your old natural *sin nature* is supernaturally changed for a new *divine nature*. A consequence of this new identity is a *new worth* based on the abundant resources placed into your personal account. A second consequence is a *new destination* throughout eternity where you will forever be secure in the presence of God.

Precious one, how God desires that you receive all that He provides! The struggle with low self-worth can actually be replaced with godly self-worth when you are in Christ. But in order for you to have the characteristics of Christ, you must be in a different family. Has that change become a reality for you? If not, on the authority of the Word of God you can become a child of God. John 1:12 says, *"To all who received him, to those who believed in his name, he gave the right to become children of God."*

If you desire this new relationship with God through Christ, you may pray this prayer:

> *Lord, I admit that many times I have chosen wrong. I know I've sinned, and I'm asking You to forgive me for my sins. I now want to become a child of God. I'm asking that Jesus Christ come into my life to be my Savior and Lord. I yield my will to His will. And I thank You for whatever He wants to make of me. In Christ's name I pray. Amen.*

In fullest humility, you can thank God for His heart's desire to move you into a new family—His family. How extraordinary—every child of God genuinely has a new worth, a new destination and a new identity! Now . . . begin to see yourself through God's eyes!

Your New Life in Christ

"For as in Adam all die, so in Christ all will be made alive." (1 Corinthians 15:22)			
"For as in Adam all die . . .		**so in Christ all will be made alive."**	
In Adam		*In Christ*	
Old creature	2 Corinthians 5:17	New creature	2 Corinthians 5:17
Unrepentant heart	Romans 2:5	New heart	Ezekiel 36:26
Slave to sin	Romans 6:6	Free from sin	Romans 6:7
Death	Romans 6:23	Life	Romans 6:22
Powerless	Romans 5:6	Strength	Philippians 4:13
Enemies of God	Romans 5:10	Reconciled to God	Romans 5:10
Condemned	Romans 5:6	No condemnation	Romans 8:1
Slave	Galatians 4:7	Son	Galatians 4:7
Slave to impurity	Romans 6:19	Slave to righteousness	Romans 6:19
Poverty	2 Corinthians 8:9	Riches	2 Corinthians 8:9
Accused	Colossians 1:22	Blameless	Colossians 1:22
Under law	Romans 6:14	Under grace	Romans 6:14
Under judgment	Romans 5:16	Justified	Romans 5:16
Under a curse	Galatians 3:13	Redeemed from curse	Galatians 3:13
Under wrath	Ephesians 2:3	Free from wrath	Romans 5:9
In darkness	Ephesians 5:8	In the light	Ephesians 5:8

"'For I know the plans I have for you,' declares the
LORD, 'plans to prosper you and not to harm you,
plans to give you hope and a future.'"
(Jeremiah 29:11)

Discovering How God Sees You

"If you call out for insight and cry aloud for understanding, and
if you look for it as for silver and search for it as for hidden
treasure, then you will . . . find the knowledge of God."
(Proverbs 2:3-5)

You are about to unearth the most priceless of all hidden treasures. To begin this great discovery, all you need is a pen and your favorite Bible translation. As you bring to the surface the truths of each daily devotion, you will see God's perspective of you from His Word.

Research has shown that it takes three weeks to form a habit; therefore, as you end this study, you should be in a precious pattern of seeing yourself through God's eyes. The following six steps will be used by the Spirit of God to bring to light that which may be currently hidden from view:

1. Begin each day asking God to reveal your worth . . . simply because you are His child.
2. Concentrate on the initial statement concerning you and on the corresponding Scripture.
3. Read the practical commentary along with the prayer that the Lord's heavenly view of you would penetrate your heart.
4. Look up the additional Scripture references from your favorite translation. Then personalize and paraphrase them, putting them into your own words.
5. Write a personal prayer completing the phrase—*Father, through Your eyes I can see that I . . .*
6. Repeat the printed truth at the bottom of the page. With a grateful heart, acknowledge that indeed God does see you as worthy of confidence and secure in value.

Day 32

I am given the compassion of Christ.

Personalize these verses in your own words.

Isaiah 49:15 *No matter who rejects me, the Lord will never forget me. No matter who is cold toward me, the Lord has compassion for me, even greater than a mother for her child.*

Lamentations 3: 22-23 *God not only loves me, He also has great compassion for me. I don't need to be overcome by my trials because God will always love me and be faithful to me.*

Father, through Your eyes I can see that I . . . *will never be without Your love and compassion. I shouldn't base how I feel about myself on how I am being treated by others. Thank You that Your compassion will never fail me.*

I am loved because . . . I have the unfailing compassion of Christ.

My Position
in Christ

"How great is the love the Father has lavished on us, that we should be called children of God!"
(1 John 3:1)

Day 1

I am adopted by God.

"He predestined us to be adopted."
(Ephesians 1:5)

Oh, to be secure! Everyone wants it; everyone longs for it. Why? Perhaps security has added significance because we all know the feeling of having the proverbial "rug pulled out from under us" by someone we've trusted. At one time, we had a home in that heart, yet the feeling of rejection sent us into feeling emotionally abandoned.

Is there a place you can call "home" and not question its future? A place of emotional security? Consider what your heavenly Father has said: "*I have adopted you.*"

Even though God already has a Son, He chooses to adopt you. God does not *have* to adopt you; He *wants* you! You are His child. . . . He is your loving Father.

Thomas Watson expressed it this way: "Since God has a Son of His own, and such a Son, how wonderful God's love in adopting us! We needed a Father, but He did not need sons."

If you have not had a meaningful relationship with your earthly father, it may be hard for you to fully comprehend a caring, loving heavenly Father. Unlike some earthly fathers, God is always available to you. He will neither leave you nor forsake you—He is with you all the time. He desires to be intimately involved in every aspect of your life. By adopting you, He has chosen you to have the full privilege of being His own.

Many similarities can be seen between God's adoption of us and the legal adoption of a child. An adopted child is not inferior to any other child in the family. An adopted child carries the family name, and his inheritance is secure because he, too, is a legal heir.

However, there is one difference. The legally adopted child will not receive the same nature as his newly adoptive parents, who have different biological genes and characteristics. Yet, in God's adoption, the child always receives a *new nature*—the nature of his heavenly Father.

History tells us that when the New Testament was written, it was understood that an adoption would never be revoked. Do you realize what that means in light of your relationship with God? *Once you are selected, you can never be rejected.* You will never be emotionally abandoned. You will always have a home in God's heart. Seeing yourself through God's eyes, you are His child *forever.*

Personalize these verses in your own words:

Romans 8:15 _____

_____

_____

_____

_____

_____

_____

Galatians 4:5-7 _____

_____

_____

_____

_____

_____

_____

Father, through Your eyes I can see that I . . . _____

_____

_____

_____

_____

_____

_____

I am secure because . . . I am adopted by God.

Day 2

I am a child of God.

"How great is the love the Father has lavished on us,
that we should be called children of God!"
(1 John 3:1)

What a tender scene . . . Jesus with the children! His disciples felt they were a nuisance, yet Jesus recognized their needs and welcomed their nearness. *"Let the little children come to me, and do not hinder them, for the kingdom of heaven belongs to such as these"* (Matthew 19:14).

Perhaps you experienced an unhappy childhood and grew up in a situation where you felt unloved. Such an experience can profoundly affect your life—even as an adult—and can result in a long, continuing search for love and acceptance.

Perhaps you've felt like a nuisance . . . unwanted and unwelcomed. It is no small matter that your heavenly Father calls you His child—a loving term of endearment. Dear child of God, you *are* loved, you *are* wanted and you *do* belong. The very "longing to belong" is put there by God Himself. He is moving to create a desire in your heart to know Him as your loving Father.

You may have heard the phrase, "*Everyone* is a child of God." While that sounds warm and wonderful, it is simply not true! According to John 1:12, "*To all who received him [Jesus Christ], to those who believed in his name, he gave the right to become children of God.*"

While the Bible teaches that everyone on earth is a *creation* of God, only those who *receive* Jesus as Lord and Savior become authentic children of God.

If a child you had never seen strolled into your house, headed for the refrigerator, made a sandwich and plopped down on the sofa, what would you do? How long would you permit this intruder to be comfortable in your home? Not long!

Yet, if your own child walked in, headed for the refrigerator, made a sandwich and so forth . . . you probably wouldn't think much about it.

Since the child belongs there, he has the right to be comfortable at home. As a part of your family, he has family privileges.

The same is true for you as a child of God. You are part of His family. He delights to provide for your needs, and as His child, you can look to Him to meet your needs. You can come into His presence at anytime. Seeing yourself through God's eyes, you are welcomed, you are wanted.

You are "at home" in God's family.

Personalize these verses in your own words:

Romans 8:16 _____

_____
_____
_____
_____
_____
_____

Ephesians 2:19 _____

_____
_____
_____
_____
_____
_____

Father, through Your eyes I can see that I . . . _____

_____
_____
_____
_____
_____

I am secure because . . . I am a child of God.

Day 3

I am precious to God.

"You are precious and honored in my sight, and . . . I love you."
(Isaiah 43:4)

Does anyone care? Do I make a difference in anyone's life? Do I matter at all? When the answers seem bleak, it's important to realize that although few have escaped the painful rocks of rejection, a shipwrecked soul is not at the heart of God's plan for any child of His. When trials seem unending, when heartaches are hitting wave upon wave, if only we could remember, "This too will pass." He says, *"You are precious and honored in my sight."*

Do you feel precious to God? Do you consider yourself cherished? Even when you feel you are not, *you truly are.* Though you've been drenched with defeat, God's love is like the endless tide. Your compassionate Savior wants you to *". . . know that the testing of your faith develops perseverance. Perseverance must finish its work so that you may be mature and complete, not lacking anything"* (James 1:2-4).

One of life's most beautiful and costly wonders is born out of pain and irritation—the pearl. When a piece of sand slips through the opening of the oyster's shell, it immediately begins to rub against the soft tissue to produce a hard substance. That hard substance eventually develops into one of the world's exquisite gems—a lovely, luminous pearl. In fact, the greater the irritation, the more valuable the pearl!

Perhaps a "grain of sand" or an excruciating trial is causing you painful irritation right now. Know that God has not abandoned you. He has a purpose in allowing trials to invade your life. God's plan for you is a perfect plan—to produce a pearl of great value. Even in the midst of the storm, you are safe. Your Savior will keep you safe from the storm's destruction.

"We are safer in the storm God sends us, than in a calm when we are befriended by the world." —Jeremy Taylor

Because of the trials you suffer, God can produce in you a quality that could not be cultivated in any other way. As you see yourself through

God's eyes, know that you are of great value to Him and that He desires the very best for you. He says, *"You are precious and honored in My sight, and . . . I love you."*

Personalize these verses in your own words:

Isaiah 43:2 _____

_____

_____

_____

_____

_____

_____

Jeremiah 29:11 _____

_____

_____

_____

_____

_____

_____

Father, through Your eyes I can see that I . . . _____

_____

_____

_____

_____

_____

_____

I am secure because . . . I am precious in the sight of God.

Day 4

I am called by name by God.

"I have summoned you by name; you are mine."
(Isaiah 43:1)

Have you ever arrived at an airport, train station or special event and found no one was there to welcome you . . . to call you by name? Have you ever rushed home with anxious anticipation to share exciting news, only to find an empty house and a deafening silence? In the depths of your being you have a need to feel that you are personally known, lovingly cared about and personally called by name.

Even though it had been several months since I had spoken and sung at a particular Christian retreat, the stinging comments from one significant person had produced acute pain. I was still smarting, as if from a bee sting! When you are stung by a bee, the sting catches you by surprise—the stinger remains, the swelling begins, the skin reddens and the area is sensitive to touch. My heart felt that same painful sensitivity as I planned to fly back to that location. Although mentally I had been preparing myself for the return, I still had a full-blown case of fear—fear that I would be hurt again.

A week prior to my departure, I mailed a note to someone who had been especially concerned about me during my time of hurt. I didn't ask her to pick me up, but I did include my flight schedule with the deep hope that she would read between the lines and be there upon my arrival.

As I deplaned, my eyes searched the airport waiting area for a familiar face. I wanted to hear a warm, "Hi, June!" but the silence from a swarming crowd echoed in my ears. Even though I had tried to prepare myself, my heart sank.

Starting toward the baggage area, I suddenly heard a voice . . . someone called out my name. Thank You, Lord, she *was* there! She had been on the observation deck long before the plane had arrived. And now she was *calling me by name*. Her calling said, "I care about you." Her words acted as a healing balm to soothe my sensitive heart.

When situations in your life begin to sting, don't assume God has forgotten you. He is still watching over you. As you see yourself through God's eyes, realize that your Lord is always there. . . . He is intimately involved in your life. . . . You are constantly on His mind. He says, *"Fear not . . . I have [called] you by name; you are mine."*

"He who counts the stars, and calls them by their names, is in no danger of forgetting His own children. He knows your case as thoroughly as if you were the only creature He ever made, or the only saint He ever loved."[1] —Charles Hadden Spurgeon

Personalize these verses in your own words:

Psalm 139:13-16 _____

_____

_____

_____

_____

_____

_____

_____

_____

_____

_____

Father, through Your eyes I can see that I . . . _____

_____

_____

_____

_____

_____

I am secure because . . . I am called by name by God.

Day 5

I am accepted by God.

"He hath made us accepted in the beloved [Jesus]."
(Ephesians 1:6, KJV)

Many people have a recording in their minds that plays the same song over and over again. The title? "If Only." The air play? Top 10! Not just for weeks, but for years. The most distinguishing feature of this song is its brevity—only one line long. "If only _____ (you fill in the blank), then I might have pleased my dad." "If only I had been smarter in school . . . been better in sports . . . been my brother . . . been born first . . . not been born at all!"

We don't understand why this one line song continues to play after the passing of time. Yet if we were to listen to recordings of some of our earliest childhood experiences, we could see why we are emotionally stuck.

The child who hears, "You'll never amount to anything," won't feel worth much. The child who hears, "I wish you had never been born," becomes performance based throughout life, trying to prove his importance to everyone in order to gain acceptance. Perhaps the perceived "If it weren't for you, I'd be happy" theme is the most melancholy melody of all. It damages a child of any age.

Dr. Charles Stanley says that most of us value the acceptance of our parents more than the acceptance of any other individual. He cites businessmen in their 40s, 50s and even 60s who are still seeking their father's acceptance and approval even though their fathers are dead. The little boy inside still cries out, *I've got to get my dad to accept me.*

While we all make mistakes, in God's eyes *you are no mistake.* As a child of God, *you are never unacceptable to Him.* He says, *"Never will I leave you; never will I forsake you"* (Hebrews 13:5).

Jesus understands your innermost feelings when you've been rejected. He personally experienced that same kind of rejection from His family. *"He came to his own, and his own received him not"* (John 1:11, KJV). Therefore, who can better empathize with your need for acceptance than your Lord!

His love and acceptance is not, "Because. . . ." He loves and accepts you, *period!* When you know you are totally *accepted in the beloved* and see yourself through God's eyes, you step to a new song of joy and acceptance as you recall this simple but classic masterpiece:

> *Jesus loves me! This I know, for the Bible tells me so.*
> *Jesus loves me! He will stay close beside me all the way.*[2]

Personalize these verses in your own words:

Psalm 27:10 _____

_____

_____

_____

_____

Jeremiah 31:3 _____

_____

_____

_____

_____

Father, through Your eyes I can see that I . . . _____

_____

_____

_____

_____

_____

I am secure because . . . I am accepted in the beloved.

Day 6

I am baptized with Christ.

"We were therefore buried with him
through baptism into death."
(Romans 6:4)

The little girl had no one with whom she could identify. She wanted to find her family but didn't know how. She searched with all her might.

> *Somewhere over the rainbow way up high,*
> *There's a land that I heard of once in a lullaby. . . .*[3]

In 1939 millions of people flocked to see the unveiling of the first motion picture to be filmed in both black and white and "living color." *The Wizard of Oz* featured colors woven throughout the fabric of the story. The motion picture industry would never be the same—this rainbow of colors gave it an exciting *new identity*.

In a similar way, one who is baptized in Christ will never be the same. The word *baptism* is black and white for many people. To others, its image has become a muddy gray . . . a mixture of misunderstanding. Yet when you correctly understand the meaning of *baptizo*, the Greek verb for "baptize," you will see a panorama of living color unfold before your very eyes.

In ancient everyday living, a piece of cloth would be immersed (*baptizo*) into a dye, a process that resulted in a *change of identity*. A bland muslin fabric would be transformed into a brilliant blue or radiant red cloth suitable for any number of important uses.

Do you realize that when you were "buried with Christ through baptism," you actually received a *change of identity?* Although you are still made of the same material, your new identity with Christ permeates the very fabric of your soul.

Your *spiritual* baptism takes place the moment you are saved, as you are instantaneously identified with Christ. Later, *water* baptism takes place as a symbol of what has happened to you.

Your water baptism symbolizes a progression of three pictures:

- Standing in the water represents your old life.
- Being lowered under the water represents death to your old life—the washing away of your sins.
- Being lifted up out of the water represents your new life in Christ.

You are now baptized into Christ, and you are lifted into a colorful new life . . . into a new family . . . *into a new identity* . . . you can see yourself through God's eyes.

Personalize these verses in your own words:

Galatians 3:26-27 _____

_____

_____

_____

_____

_____

Colossians 2:9-12 _____

_____

_____

_____

_____

_____

Father, through Your eyes I can see that I . . . _____

_____

_____

_____

_____

_____

I am secure because . . . I am now identified with Christ.

Day 7

I am hidden with Christ.

"You are my hiding place; you will protect me from trouble."
(Psalm 32:7)

The Nazis wielded terror over all who were not like them in race, religion or rule. During World War II, the primary hate targets were the Jews: their power was stripped, property confiscated, people confined—and killed—in concentration camps. In fact, in Nazi dominated Holland, the Ten Boom family had carefully hidden hundreds of Jews in their "hiding place"—the secret place in their home above their watch shop.

Then on February 28, 1944, that which was most feared happened—the hiding place was discovered! The Gestapo arrested the Ten Boom family. Their crime? Hiding Jews. Their punishment? Immediate transport to a concentration camp.

As the two sisters waited in line to be searched, Corrie asked God if He would keep the Bible that was tucked inside her clothing hidden from view. "Dear God . . . You have given me this precious Book, You have kept it hidden through checkpoints and inspections." The woman in front of Corrie was searched three times. Corrie's beloved sister Betsie, standing behind her, was also searched. Miraculously, the officer never touched Corrie. Her Bible now had a hiding place in a German concentration camp![4]

Filth, disease, beatings and rape became a part of their struggle for survival. But as Corrie read the Bible's truths, she knew His Word would keep hatred from her heart. *"I have hidden your word in my heart that I might not sin against you"* (Psalm 119:11).

Is there a hiding place for you? A place of healing for your damaged emotions? When you have been treated harshly, you can be free of hatred. Because He hides His truth in you, you are protected from wrong thoughts and wrong choices. The adversary of your life has no power to trap you . . . as long as you stay hidden in the shelter of God's wings where you are safe from emotional destruction, hidden from emotional ruin.

The Ten Boom family had their hiding place only for a while. But as God's child, you are hidden in Christ. Seeing yourself through God's eyes, you can know that you are safe forever!

Under His wings, what a refuge in sorrow!
How the heart yearningly turns to His rest!
Often when earth has no balm for my healing,
There I find comfort and there I am blest.[5]

Personalize these verses in your own words:

Psalm 17:8 _____

_____

_____

_____

_____

_____

Colossians 3:3 _____

_____

_____

_____

_____

_____

Father, through Your eyes I can see that I . . . _____

_____

_____

_____

_____

_____

_____

I am secure because . . . I am hidden with Christ.

His Plan
for Me

"'Come now, let us reason together,' says the LORD. 'Though your sins are like scarlet, they shall be as white as snow; though they are red as crimson, they shall be like wool.'"
(Isaiah 1:18)

Day 8

I am chosen by God.

"He chose us in him before the creation of the world."
(Ephesians 1:4)

School was in session, and everything was fine . . . fine until it was time for teams to be chosen. As the team captains called out the names of their chosen players, the air filled with awkwardness—at least for one timid teenager who was anything but agile. *Oh God, I hate being chosen last. Please let somebody want me.*

Have you ever longed to be chosen because you were wanted . . . because you were desired? Child of God, the Lord chose you *"before the creation of the world."* He chose you only because He wanted you—not because of your strength, scholarship or skill. We can take no credit or merit in being chosen. Jesus clearly states, *"You did not choose me, but I chose you"* (John 15:16).

Many years ago another child faced being chosen. The Lord sent the prophet Samuel to Jesse of Bethlehem saying, *"I have chosen one of his sons to be king"* (1 Samuel 16:1). What an unfathomable honor for a family! Yet after Samuel had surveyed Jesse's seven sons, he said, *"The Lord has not chosen these. . . . Are these all the sons you have?"* (1 Samuel 16:10-11). Well, there was David, the youngest. But he was away tending sheep—and certainly not "king material"! At the prophet's insistence, however, the lad was brought in. Immediately, the Lord told Samuel to choose David, *"and from that day on the Spirit of the LORD came upon David in power"* (1 Samuel 16:13).

In a most crucial battle we see Goliath completely terrorizing Saul's army. However, God uses the young, inexperienced David as the man of the hour. Imagine the Israelites' amazement as they watch "unarmored" David approaching Goliath. Just how could this child be confident of conquest? David knew the simple principle: whatever God *chooses* for you to do, He will *equip* you to do. In a moment, David single-handedly slew the nine-foot titan. His secret? He understood the true source of strength, declaring before the confrontation, *"The battle is the LORD's"* (1 Samuel 17:47).

What truth for you today! When you face the "Goliaths" in your life, remember this: you have been chosen *by* the Lord. As you now see yourself through God's eyes, have confidence *in* the Lord—the battle is the Lord's!

Personalize these verses in your own words:

John 15:19 _____

_____

_____

_____

_____

_____

_____

Romans 8:33 _____

_____

_____

_____

_____

_____

Father, through Your eyes I can see that I . . . _____

_____

_____

_____

_____

_____

I have confidence because . . . I am chosen by God.

Day 9

I am born again by God.

"You must be born again."
(John 3:7)

No sentence in Scripture has been subjected to more contemporary cynicism, sarcasm and satire than the impossible sounding, *"You must be born again."* Born again? Jesus left no other option. He said it is a *must!* But why?

In God's original creation, Adam and Eve were made in the "image" of God. Since *"God is spirit"* (John 4:24), the image was actually God's Spirit alive in them. Their human spirits were indwelled by the Holy Spirit, resulting in a oneness of mind and heart. But when sin came in, the Spirit went out. Oneness was broken. Adam and Eve became *spiritually dead.* Likewise, all who were born after them were born *dead in their sins.*

Upon your physical birth you were born in sin, born lost, born alienated, born an enemy of God, born spiritually dead. What is the only thing a dead person needs? Life! Not sincerity or education, culture or finances or even religion. What you need is life.

Spiritually, when you accept God's plan of salvation, you go from death to life. You receive Christ's life! As a result, you are given a new nature—His nature. You are given a new spirit—His Spirit.

The phrase "born again" in Greek literally means "born anew, born from above." This indicates that when the Spirit of God so transforms a life, it can only be described as a dramatic "new birth." Oh, child of God, marvel at the beauty of being *born from above!*

The critic says, "Impossible! How can a person be born again?" Yet in nature, God has given us the little caterpillar to unravel this mystery for the whole world to see. This drab and dull creature worms its way through life until it dies to its caterpillar existence. But then the impossible occurs! The death of the caterpillar brings forth the birth of the butterfly. Behold—the miracle of the monarch! A two-inch worm unfolds a four-inch wing span . . . pallid, pale green is transformed into regal, reddish gold . . . a former creeping crawler begins an "impossible" migratory trip—nearly 2,000 miles in flight!

So it is when you are born anew that you can see yourself through God's eyes. The old is gone, the new is alive to soar to heights unknown.

Now, spread your wings child of God . . . soar to new heights!

Personalize these verses in your own words:

2 Corinthians 5:17

_____

_____

_____

_____

_____

_____

1 Peter 1:3, 23

_____

_____

_____

_____

_____

_____

Father, through Your eyes I can see that I . . .

_____

_____

_____

_____

_____

_____

I have confidence because . . . I am born anew by God.

Day 10

I am saved by God.

*"For it is by grace you have been saved, through faith—
and this not from yourselves, it is the gift of God."*
(Ephesians 2:8)

My brother's family was excited about moving into their new home. The carpet was down, the curtains were up, the furniture was in. Only a few items remained to be moved. Then in the early morning just before the family was to take up residence, a fire broke out, and their possessions went up in flames. Personal items, precious mementos and priceless pictures were all lost.

When I arrived at the charred frame, I had expected to see my brother. Instead, he and his family had gone to the homes of two firemen who, to my horror, had lost their lives in the blaze. The deepest desire of all our hearts was, *If only they could have been saved.* Only against such a black backdrop could the significance of salvation be so desperately real.

Saved . . . who wouldn't want to be saved? The word *saved* obviously implies being saved *from* something. Oh, if all humanity would comprehend what Scripture says they can be saved *from:* an eternal existence of complete anguish, a destiny of living in darkness. Who wouldn't want deliverance?

Just think—you were delivered from this dominion of darkness. The Greek word for *saved* means "to be delivered, to be preserved." This is the eternal benefit resulting from your decision to accept Christ's offer of salvation.

But the scope of spiritual salvation doesn't extend just to being saved from the *penalty* of sin. As a child of God, you are also saved from the *power* of sin. You are actually "dead to sin" (Romans 6:11). Simply put, you can break free from any sinful habit! And that's not all. One day, in heaven, you will be saved from the very *presence* of sin.

For me, however, the most phenomenal aspect of salvation is not what we've been saved *from*, but rather what we've been saved *for*. God's heart desire is not just to get us *out* of hell, but to get the Savior *into* us.

With His presence in you, you have His power, His wisdom, His forgiveness, His love and His strength. It is His life *in* you, living His life *through* you!

What incredible value! And the amazing fact is that it's a free gift. But it's not cheap. It cost Christ His life. Salvation is a free gift to you and me because Someone else paid for it, and you now can see yourself through God's eyes.

Personalize these verses in your own words:

Exodus 15:2 _____

_____

_____

_____

_____

_____

_____

Hebrews 7:25 _____

_____

_____

_____

_____

_____

Father, through Your eyes I can see that I . . . _____

_____

_____

_____

_____

I have confidence because . . . I am saved by God's grace.

Day 11

I am justified by God.

"You were justified in the name of the Lord Jesus Christ."
(1 Corinthians 6:11)

Have you ever been on trial? There you stand in life's courtroom of criticism and accusation. Devastated, you face enemies sitting in the role of judge and jury. How is it that others can have such control over events that shape your life? How can you deal with the pain of unwarranted faultfinding and unjustified conclusions? What is your position when condemned and determined to be guilty by these self-appointed critics?

The most extraordinary day of your Christian life is the day when you are on trial. Your rightful Judge brings down the gavel and proclaims you *justified.* God uses a legal term that means, "acquitted, vindicated, declared righteous." A popular amplification for justified is *just-as-if-I'd* never sinned.

Imagine yourself in a court of law. The judge has heard the testimony of the highway patrol officer. He has determined you are guilty of speeding and firmly pronounces a mandatory fine of $100. Then a most unexpected thing happens, causing a stir in the courtroom. The judge rises, steps down from the bench and takes off his robe. Opening his wallet, he counts out the correct currency and pays your fine! This judge happens to be your father. As a judge, he must make sure that justice is served as he applies the law of the land to your actions. But as a father, he demonstrates the love in his heart, pays your penalty and buys your freedom.

This scene portrays what your heavenly Father did for you. As a *just* God, He has to sentence you to death because of your sins. But as a *loving Father,* He provided the payment for your sins—and you received life. Jesus was the payment. His death bought you life. His death paid the price.

When you yield control of your life to Christ, you are more than pardoned. A pardoned sinner is simply excused from the penalty of sin, but the charge is still recorded. However, when you are justified, you receive total acquittal not only from all obligation, but also from all accusation! The charge is erased from the "record book of life." On every charge brought against you, the Judge has spoken, and no one can reverse His divine decision. As you see yourself through God's eyes, you realize that you are "acquitted! vindicated! justified!"

Personalize these verses in your own words:

Romans 5:1 _____

_____

_____

_____

_____

_____

_____

Galatians 2:16 _____

_____

_____

_____

_____

_____

Father, through Your eyes I can see that I . . . _____

_____

_____

_____

_____

_____

I have confidence because . . . I am justified by God.

Day 12

I am redeemed by God.

"Christ redeemed us."
(Galatians 3:13)

In March of 1932, the entire world grieved with the Charles Lindbergh family when their 20-month-old son was kidnapped. Little Charles, Jr. was abducted from his home and held for $50,000 ransom. Aviator Lindbergh had become an international hero after making the first transatlantic flight in 1927. However, his fame did not protect his child from danger. Neither did it protect him from the desperate desire to pay the ransom. Yet, even with the full ransom paid, the Lindberghs found themselves victimized—powerless to change the evil travesty. Their baby was cruelly killed by the kidnapper.

The world's first abduction was carried out in a garden setting. Eden was the perfect haven provided by God for all mankind. With cunning cleverness, the adversary-kidnapper tempted and lured the innocent pair into sin and thereby made hostages of all who were to follow. Alienated from home, sentenced to separation and death, the only hope of the human race was "to be released on receipt of the ransom."

Unlike the Lindberghs, who could not save their child, the heavenly Father sent His son, Jesus Christ, to *redeem* you—His child—by paying the full ransom with His life. His death purchased your life! The price? His shed blood.

The two Greek verbs translated *redeemed* mean "to release on receipt of a ransom" or "to buy out." Bible scholar Lawrence Richards explains that *redeemed* is set "against the background of helplessness . . . human beings captured, held captive by the power forces they cannot overcome. Only by the intervention of a third party can bondage be broken and the person freed."[6]

Who, at one time or another, has not been victimized? You felt powerless to help yourself. In particular, victims of physical and emotional abuse internalize the impact of feeling powerless. The adversary-kidnapper would want to lure you with his lie, "You are a powerless prisoner, a helpless hostage." But child of God, you are *not* powerless! The hostage-taker has no control over you. God has already redeemed you. Christ paid your ransom in full.

As Jesus proclaimed, *"If the Son sets you free, you will be free indeed"* (John 8:36). As you see yourself through God's eyes, you realize that you've been redeemed in the most valuable ransom exchange in the history of the world—the Perfect Lamb bought your freedom.

Personalize these verses in your own words:

Matthew 20:28 _____

_____

_____

_____

_____

_____

_____

1 Corinthians 6:19-20 _____

_____

_____

_____

_____

_____

_____

Father, through Your eyes I can see that I . . . _____

_____

_____

_____

_____

_____

I have confidence because . . . I am redeemed by God.

Day 13

I am forgiven by God.

"Blessed is he whose transgressions are forgiven."
(Psalm 32:1)

Have you ever felt the weight of choosing wrong . . . then the doubled weight of another's unforgiveness? Heaviness resides in the heart of the unforgiven.

Forgiveness is liberating—it lightens the load of both the forgiven and the forgiver. One of the Greek words for *forgiveness* means to "loose away from, lift off, release." Imagine a cluster of red helium balloons being released into the air, never to be seen again.

But a balloon cannot fly away when the string is tied to a heavy weight. Your sins create a heavy weight, one that you cannot remove. When you trust Jesus Christ as your Savior, God cuts the string, removes the weight and your sins fly away—you are forgiven! God forgives your sins through Christ's death. He "releases" the burden of wrong and sends it away.

It grieves us to realize that every wrong word, every wrong act and every wrong thought is marked down on a divine ledger sheet. God sees them all—even the things you thought no one else knew. He not only sees your actions, but also knows your heart. Hebrews 4:13 says, *"Nothing in all creation is hidden from God's sight. Everything is uncovered and laid bare before the eyes of him to whom we must give account."*

Oh, the freedom of forgiveness when you, as a child of God, realize that Jesus erased your ledger! That is why forgiveness is so totally liberating. As He hung dying on the cross, His blood was the payment for your wrong. Written across the ledger was *tetelestai* (Greek), which means "paid in full." Unlike our human forgiveness, which is often forgiving but not forgetting, God has the capacity to instantly forgive you and remember your sins no more! Psalm 103:12 gives the assurance, *"As far as the east is from the west, so far has he removed our transgressions from us."*

As you see yourself through God's eyes, you are liberated! Your guilt is gone. Your sin will not be seen again . . . your heaviness is lifted, your heart is *released*. There truly is freedom in forgiveness.

Personalize these verses in your own words:

1 John 1:9
_____

_____
_____
_____
_____
_____
_____

Hebrews 8:12
_____

_____
_____
_____
_____
_____

Father, through Your eyes I can see that I . . .
_____

_____
_____
_____
_____
_____

I have confidence because . . . I am forgiven by God.

Day 14

I am washed by God.

"Cleanse me with hyssop, and I will be clean;
wash me, and I will be whiter than snow."
(Psalm 51:7)

I remember a snowfall so clean and clear, so pure and perfectly white. The silent invitation to step into the new fallen snow was irresistible. As I walked, I marveled at the soft snow blanketing the lawns and bushes. It was as though nature had been cleansed of all imperfections. On returning from my walk, however, I was saddened by the muddy tracks I had made. The ugly dirt underneath the pure snow had left its stain. No longer did the scene display a portrait so appealing.

The next morning, to my delight, God had quietly and lovingly covered the muddy track with a fresh new blanket of snow. There was no sign of the intruding walk I had taken the day before.

A fresh new day—a fresh new start.

Do you feel that the landscape of your life is hopelessly marred by the muddy footprints of failure? Do you grieve with never-ending guilt because you stepped into sin and found yourself soiled and stained? "If only I could start over . . ." but you can't forgive yourself. Child of God, do you realize that at the time of your salvation you were given both a fresh new heart and a fresh new start? You were cleansed and made "whiter than snow."

Over a century ago, a hymn writer captured in melodious poetry the cleansing that took place in your heart when your sin was washed away:

> *Lord Jesus, I long to be perfectly whole;*
> *I want Thee forever to live in my soul.*
> *Break down every idol, cast out every foe;*
> *Now wash me and I shall be whiter than snow.*
> *Whiter than snow, whiter than snow,*
> *Lord wash me and I will be whiter than snow.*[7]

Since the Lord has cleansed you, you no longer carry the stain of sin. You have been covered by His blanket of holiness. Your sins are forgiven, never to be held against you. *"'Come now, let us reason together,' says the LORD. 'Though your sins are like scarlet, they shall be as white as snow'"* (Isaiah 1:18).

By seeing yourself through God's eyes, you can view each day as a fresh new day, a fresh new start!

Personalize these verses in your own words:

Psalm 51:10 _____

_____

_____

_____

_____

_____

Ezekiel 36:25 _____

_____

_____

_____

_____

_____

Father, through Your eyes I can see that I . . . _____

_____

_____

_____

_____

_____

_____

I have confidence because . . . I am
washed whiter than snow.

Day 15

I am reconciled to God.

"We were reconciled to him through the death of his Son."
(Romans 5:10)

Has your heart ever been broken over a shattered relationship? The closeness cut, a specialness severed? No matter how hard you tried, you couldn't force the relationship to be reconciled. The pain of someone so dear taking on the form of your "enemy" was more than you could bear. You prayed for things to be different—for the clock to be turned back—for the opportunity to recapture what once had been.

Whether the broken relationship is between parent and child, husband and wife, or friend and friend, the heart has a longing to be *reconciled*. What a word of hope! The Greek word translated *reconciled* means "to change thoroughly, to exchange from one condition to another." Reconciliation means that a personal relationship is changed; the heart of hostility is *exchanged* for a heart of harmony.

Sin destroys our harmonious relationship with God. It causes our hearts to be hostile toward Him. In reconciling us to Himself, the Father *changes* our "enemy" hearts so that we can enjoy friendship with Him.

No other illustration portrays God's heart of reconciliation more perfectly than that of The Prodigal Son, often called the most beautiful short story ever written. In Luke chapter 15 an ungrateful younger son demands and receives his inheritance from his loving father. After quickly wasting his fortune, he awakens one day in the gutter. Friends and money gone, he finds a job feeding pigs. *Feeding pigs*—the most disgraceful job a Jewish boy could have! Finally, coming to his senses, he realizes his unworthiness and heads home, hoping only to be hired as a servant. But can he go home?

What a perfect setup for a father to say, "I told you so!" But not this father. Instead, upon seeing his wayward son in the distance, he is filled with compassion and runs to embrace the broken, repentant prodigal, exclaiming, *"This son of mine was dead and is alive again!"* (Luke 15:24).

Do you realize that your compassionate Father is waiting with open arms for your heart to be changed toward Him? What joy floods His heart the day you are reconciled to Him. Seeing yourself through God's eyes, you now enjoy friendship with God.

I've wandered far away from God, now I'm coming home.
The paths of sin too long I've trod, now I'm coming home.
Coming home, coming home, never more to roam,
Open wide Thine arms of love, Lord, I'm coming home.[8]

Personalize these verses in your own words:

Romans 5:10 _____

_____

_____

_____

_____

_____

Colossians 1:22 _____

_____

_____

_____

_____

Father, through Your eyes I can see that I . . . _____

_____

_____

_____

_____

_____

I have confidence because . . . I am reconciled to God.

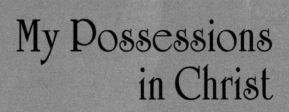

My Possessions
in Christ

"He gives strength to the weary and increases the power of the weak. Even youths grow tired and weary, and young men stumble and fall; but those who hope in the LORD will renew their strength. They will soar on wings like eagles; they will run and not grow weary, they will walk and not be faint."
(Isaiah 40:29-31)

Day 16

I am given a new heart by God.

"I will give you a new heart and put a new spirit in you."
(Ezekiel 36:26)

Many years ago, a friend brought me a clock from Switzerland. It was cleverly designed with a little bird peeking out of its tiny house. But it wasn't very useful—the clock didn't keep the time correctly. It would "cuckoo" when it wasn't supposed to! Because I loved the clock, I took it to be repaired. The clocksmith examined the inside of my cherished gift and said it needed a new mainspring. Laughingly, he told me, "Your clock needs a new heart!"

This is true for more than clocks. Every *person* needs a new heart. Just look around you. How many parents have intentionally trained their children to lie, or encouraged them to steal from another child, or to yell at another, or to hit another? Very few, if any. Yet, how many children have lied, stolen, yelled at and hit others? All have. Why? Because their hearts were self-seeking and self-centered from birth.

According to the Word of God, you were born with a sinful nature. Psalm 51:5 says, *"Surely I was sinful at birth, sinful from the time my mother conceived me."* And Jeremiah 17:9 adds, *"The heart is deceitful above all things and beyond cure."*

But the good news is that God said, *"I will give you a new heart and put a new spirit in you."* When you come into a genuine relationship with Christ, God puts a new heart inside you.

Your need is very similar to the need of someone who has a diseased heart and whose only hope for life is a heart transplant. In a spiritual sense, God takes your "diseased" heart and replaces it with a new one.

Slowly, after this divine transplant, healing begins and, as promised, your new heart becomes capable of perfect love. Your self-centeredness is now Christ-centeredness. There is healing to replace the hatred—there is a balm for bitterness. You can face the world with a freedom and a future you have never known before.

"Create in me a pure heart, O God, and renew a steadfast spirit within me" (Psalm 51:10). Once you have a changed heart, you have a changed life. Seeing yourself through God's eyes, you can love the unlovable, be kind to the unkind and forgive the unforgivable. All this because you have a new heart—you have God's heart.

Personalize these verses in your own words:

1 Timothy 1:5 _____

_____

_____

_____

_____

_____

2 Timothy 2:22 _____

_____

_____

_____

_____

_____

Father, through Your eyes I can see that I . . . _____

_____

_____

_____

_____

_____

I have worth because . . . I am given a new heart by God.

Day 17

I am given the Holy Spirit.

"We have . . . received . . . the Spirit who is from God."
(1 Corinthians 2:12)

An unexpected blackout took my neighborhood by surprise. One minute the lights were on; the next they were off. In total darkness, I inched my way to the bedside table and fumbled for the flashlight. What frustration . . . it didn't work! How useless . . . a flashlight that didn't function.

Just as useless is the person who is unable to function according to God's divine plan. Why? Because God originally designed the human spirit to contain the Holy Spirit. In the Garden, Adam and Eve had "perfect oneness" with God. The Holy Spirit indwelled their human spirits and enlightened every aspect of their lives. However, one day they pronounced their "declaration of independence" from God. Consequently, when sin came in, the Spirit went out. No Spirit, no life, no light. Like a flashlight without batteries, there was no power on the inside; so there was no light on the outside. They spiraled downward into spiritual darkness.

Yet, God did not give up on those who were born into that same darkness. *"The lamp of the LORD searches the spirit of a man"* (Proverbs 20:27). God's desire was to restore the Holy Spirit to the human spirit so that purpose and power could be restored.

Everyone knows the frustration of wandering in the dark. *Where do I go? What should I do? How am I to think?* When you are saved, you are also *"marked in him with a seal, the promised Holy Spirit"* (Ephesians 1:13). He comes in to be the illuminator of your life and enlightens your path into the future.

Because He knows all—past, present and future—He is the perfect guide for your life. *"When he, the Spirit of truth, comes, he will guide you into all truth"* (John 16:13). How? Your own personal counselor, conscience and comforter fills your soul (mind, will and emotions) with perfect truth. He teaches your mind, directs your will and controls your emotions.

Like the flashlight, you were designed to shine . . . but you can never shine with your own power. The Holy Spirit, filling your human spirit, provides the power to produce the light. As you live dependent on that power, you will shine as you were intended to shine.

Just see that in God's eyes you can never be useless when you have such relationship with Him! *You are the light of the world"* (Matthew 5:14).

Personalize these verses in your own words:

John 14:16
\
\
\
\
\
\
\

1 Corinthians 6:19
\
\
\
\
\
\
\

Father, through Your eyes I can see that I . . .
\
\
\
\
\
\
\

I have worth because . . . I am given the Holy Spirit.

Day 18

I am given the mind of Christ.

"We have the mind of Christ."
(1 Corinthians 2:16)

One cold evening the fire was warming, as was our conversation. I was spending special time with one of my closest friends—one whom I've known many years. Several times during the evening, I would start to say something and before I could get my thoughts completely formed, she would finish my sentence. Twice, I remember, we actually said the same word at the same time.

My friend and I have a unique oneness of mind and spirit. We know each other's sensitivities and sorrows . . . the preferences and the pains.

When you think of the mind of Christ, surely this is the closeness God wants you to have with Him. He wants you to know His heart by knowing His Word. He wants His thinking to saturate your thoughts. His plan from the beginning has been that His nature become your "second nature."

When you are given a new life in Christ, you are given a "new nature." *Nature* simply means doing what comes naturally. He gives you the capacity to think as He *naturally* thinks. What an extraordinary gift!

A writer friend of mine told me that every time she sits down to write, she first prays that she will have the mind of Christ—His thoughts flowing through her as she writes. Her comment had a strong impact on me . . . I now pray in the same way.

In the midst of confusion, you need the mind of Christ. In the midst of conflict, when criticism is caustic, when advice is adversarial—you need the mind of Christ. As long as you live, there will always be those who are mentally and emotionally on the attack.

Remember Job's "friends"? Although he had done nothing wrong, he was besieged with assumptions of his "sin." He was weighted down by their words, their volumes of verbiage.

At times, you may feel like Job, wondering what is true. The advice-givers go on and on weaving their webs of words. Somehow you feel caught. Can you possibly get free? As you develop the mind of Christ, you will be freed from the world's web that would keep you weighted down and entangled.

Knowing the mind of Christ comes from a shared relationship, a progressive growth and an intimate oneness with Him. Seeing yourself through God's eyes, you develop a deeper oneness of mind and spirit. There can be no greater basis for friendship!

Personalize these verses in your own words:

Romans 12:1-2 _____

_____

_____

_____

_____

_____

_____

Ephesians 4:23 _____

_____

_____

_____

_____

_____

_____

Father, through Your eyes I can see that I . . . _____

_____

_____

_____

_____

_____

I have worth because . . . I am given the mind of Christ.

Day 19

I am given strength from God.

"The LORD gives strength to his people."
(Psalm 29:11)

For thousands of years a club has been in existence offering memberships throughout the world. It's a popular club; it's a prolific club. It's the "I Can't Club."

Under the bylaws, club members are required to make "I can't" statements with conviction: "I can't help but hate after what he's done to me." "I can't quit this sin." "I can't forgive again!" Such fervor makes it sound as if each "I can't" statement is an unchangeable, universal law.

If you're a member, your pledge echoes its premise: "No one can win over sin." You believe its promise: "Defeat is normal." And you promote its purpose—to fill each mind with futility.

One law of science to which everyone is subject is the law of gravity— the force that pulls every object to the center of the earth. Likewise, the members of the "I Can't Club" are prisoners to the downward pull of defeat—not only ground-bound, but sin-bound.

Do you feel bound to a specific sin? Does quitting the "I Can't Club" seem impossible? For every child of His, the Father refuses to let *can't* be the universal password. Upon your salvation, He gives you the Spirit of God so that you will have the *strength* of God. He deals a deathblow to the "I Can't Club." He makes it possible for you to overcome any sin. How? By replacing one law for another: *"The law of the Spirit of life set me free from the law of sin and death"* (Romans 8:2).

Can you imagine a 190-ton mass of metal rising against the pull of gravity? Impossible! *It can't* be done! Oh, yes it can . . . by using a "higher law." When you, in faith, give yourself over to the principle of aerodynamics, you can enter an airplane with full confidence that it will fly you from one city to another. You are no longer ground-bound.

Similarly, when you, in faith, give yourself over to the Spirit's control, the "I can't" statements will no longer keep you from leaving the runway of life. When God fills your spirit with His Spirit and infuses you with His strength, you are no longer sin-bound. Seeing yourself through God's eyes, you see that every "I Can't" becomes "I Can!"

> *"He gives strength to the weary and increases the power of the weak.*
> *. . . But those who hope in the LORD will renew their strength.*
> *They will soar on wings like eagles."*
> *(Isaiah 40:29, 31)*

Personalize these verses in your own words:

Ephesians 3:16 _____

_____

_____

_____

_____

_____

_____

Philippians 4:13 _____

_____

_____

_____

_____

_____

Father, through Your eyes I can see that I . . . _____

_____

_____

_____

_____

I have worth because . . . I am given strength from God.

Day 20

I am given the mercy of God.

"I will have mercy on whom I will have mercy."
(Exodus 33:19)

All eyes are on the woman. Her face is masked with fear. Heart pounding, blood racing . . . her mind is frantic as the Pharisees fling her before Christ and the curious crowd. Her fate lies with them. With slanderous delight, her accusers recount how she had been caught in the act of adultery. Reminding Jesus that according to Jewish law she must be stoned, they demand, *"Now what do you say?"* (John 8:5).

But Jesus' concern is for this woman's soul rather than for her sin. He shifts the focus to the "faultless" Pharisees, stating, *"He that is without sin among you, let him first cast a stone at her"* (John 8:7, KJV). What? You mean they must scrutinize *themselves?* The Lord cut open the conscience of the crowd. One by one—in slow motion—they retreat, leaving only the woman to face the Man of mercy, the only One who could rightfully throw a stone.

"Has no one condemned you?" asks Jesus. *"Neither do I condemn [you]: go, and sin no more."* What mercy . . . Jesus, looking past her fault, seeing her need, forgiving her sin, setting her free. An adulteress deserving death is given another chance at life. What matchless mercy!

Mercy means, literally, "the outward manifestation of pity." Mercy is more than emotion; it is *active compassion* meeting a need. No one has a right to mercy. It is simply extended because of the heart of the giver and the need of the receiver. Therefore, when God extends His mercy, He naturally expresses His heart of compassion.

As His child, God has given you an invaluable coin of compassion. One side is engraved with grace; the other is minted with mercy. Throughout your life He extends both grace (*giving* you what you *do not* deserve: liberation), and mercy (*not giving* you what you *do* deserve: condemnation).

You can't buy the coin . . . it's priceless. You can't earn the coin . . . it's undeserved. In fact, you can't merit mercy; if you could, it wouldn't be mercy.

Child of God, seeing yourself through God's eyes, you can know you are forgiven—not by merit but by mercy. What compassion from the Man of mercy!

Personalize these verses in your own words:

Isaiah 55:7 _____

_____

_____

_____

_____

_____

_____

Hebrews 4:16 _____

_____

_____

_____

_____

_____

Father, through Your eyes I can see that I . . . _____

_____

_____

_____

_____

_____

_____

I have worth because . . . I am given the mercy of God.

Day 21

I am given the grace of God.

"He gives us more grace."
(James 4:6)

My all-time favorite class was ninth grade algebra. Because I loved puzzles, algebra was actually fun. Since other subjects were hard for me, my A's in algebra helped to soothe my suffering self-image. In math class, I faced each test with confidence! Tuesday's test would be no different.

But while taking the test, I suddenly found that I couldn't remember the formula for number one . . . number two, or three, four, five . . . my mind had gone blank! I could solve only the last two problems. Stunned, I handed my paper to the teacher. After a long pensive pause, she asked, "When do you have study hall tomorrow?" "At ten o'clock," I nervously replied. The next day at ten sharp, I was sitting in my algebra classroom with a second chance. I was given a gift called "grace."

Before even knowing what the word *grace* meant, I knew what it was like to be impacted by it. I was awed that a teacher would extend *undeserved favor* toward me. That's what the Greek word for grace means: "underserved care, unearned favor."

God is a God of second chances, full of grace, a God who not only saves you from eternal death, but also saves you from a defeated life. He saves you by putting His life in you. If you focus only on what it's like to fail in certain areas of your life, you could be drawn into the downward spiral of dejection. However, Jesus said, *"I have come that they might have life, and have it to the full"* (John 10:10).

> *He giveth more grace when the burden grows greater;*
> *He sendeth more strength when the labors increase.*
> *To added affliction, He addeth His mercy;*
> *To multiplied trials, His multiplied peace.*
> *His love has no limit; His grace has no measure;*
> *His pow'r has no boundary known unto men.*
> *For out of His infinite riches in Jesus,*
> *He giveth, and giveth, and giveth again!*[9]

Can you really have fullness when you have failed? Oh, child of God, discouragement, defeat and dejection are what the God of all grace can save you from. Seeing yourself through God's eyes, you will find that in your weakness, He will be your strength. In your failure, He will give you fullness.

How blessed you are to know the God of grace, who saves you from your failures. He is the God of the second chance . . . and the third . . . and the fourth . . . and the fifth. . . .

Personalize these verses in your own words:

2 Corinthians 12:9 _____

_____
_____
_____
_____
_____

2 Corinthians 9:8 _____

_____
_____
_____
_____

Father, through Your eyes I can see that I . . . _____

_____
_____
_____
_____
_____
_____

I have worth because . . . I am given the grace of God.

Day 22

I am given complete access to God.

"In him and through faith in him we may approach
God with freedom and confidence."
(Ephesians 3:12)

As you were growing up, what kind of "signs" did your father wear? Was he labeled "approachable . . . available . . . accessible"? I'll never forget my best friend's father. He wore those signs naturally and never once threatened to remove them. As a teenager, I was continually drawn to him and always felt valuable in his presence while in their home.

The life of this man, so accessible, was in sharp contrast to that of my own father, who enforced his belief that "children should be seen and not heard." I was so intimidated by his austerity that occasionally, upon hearing his footsteps, I would hide behind a door. It was never normal for me to sit in his lap, kiss his cheek or share my secrets. I felt my father wore signs that blared, "KEEP OUT . . . NO TRESPASSING . . . DO NOT ENTER!"

Each evening after dinner, my father demanded the full attention of my mother, literally forbidding her to be with us. I will always remember the loneliness of being barred from receiving my mother's care and concern night after night.

Many people think of God in the same way as I perceived my father—imposing, powerful, completely inaccessible and certainly not interested in the details of their lives.

What is true about God? How do you know what your heavenly Father is really like? In John 14:8 Philip emphatically said, *"Show us the Father."* Jesus responded, *"Anyone who has seen me, has seen the Father. . . . I am in the Father, and . . . the Father is in me"* (John 14:9-10). The truth about God can be found in Jesus.

Being accessible to the poor, Jesus did not wear fashion labels for the elite. He wore no "unapproachable" labels for the leper. Even the prostitute was moved by His openness. And when the children tried to get close to Him, Jesus rebuked His disciples for trying to pin on Him the label "Unavailable." From child to leper, from seeker to sinner, no one felt unacceptable in the presence of Jesus. Though He is Almighty God in the flesh, He is always accessible. From the beginning of time to today, God is always accessible to you!

Whether or not you have ever experienced access to a loving, earthly father, you do have complete access to your heavenly Father. Seeing yourself through God's eyes, you know that He never has a "DO NOT ENTER" sign over His heart.

Personalize these verses in your own words:

Ephesians 2:18 _____

_____

_____

_____

_____

_____

Hebrews 4:16 _____

_____

_____

_____

_____

Father, through Your eyes I can see that I . . . _____

_____

_____

_____

_____

_____

_____

I have worth because . . . I am given access to God.

Day 23

I am given everything I need by God.

"His divine power has given us everything
we need for life and godliness."
(2 Peter 1:3)

Many years ago after opening my first bank account, I remember feeling really awkward. I was given a book of checks but didn't know how to use them! How embarrassing to have money in the bank and yet not know how to get it out.

Not wanting my two younger sisters to experience this same confusion, I went to our neighborhood bank and opened checking accounts for each of them. I can still remember the exhilaration I felt as I made deposits in their names to accounts they hadn't even heard about, hadn't earned and hadn't expected. Then I told them what I had done and taught them how to draw from their resources in the bank!

What heightened joy the heavenly Father must feel when He opens your personal account in His bank, the "Blessing Bank." Open 24 hours a day, this bank offers unlimited blessings and unlimited withdrawals.

Do you realize that you actually have this spiritual bank account? The moment you become a child of God, He establishes your personal account with deposits vastly beyond your ability to exhaust. You are given every resource you will ever need to reflect the character of God within your life.

One major oversight of God's children is that they too often don't open their bankbooks to see the balance of their deposits. In reality, your bankbook, the Bible, discloses your personal assets in great detail. Are you troubled? Romans 5:1 shows your deposit of peace. Are you weak? Philippians 4:13 reveals your deposit of strength. The 2 Corinthians 5:5 entry indicates that God *"has given us the Spirit as a deposit."* And what a deposit—God on the inside reproducing His life on the outside!

Do you feel angry? Do you need patience? Open your heart to the Spirit, and check the specific Scriptures and promises He has deposited in your account to meet your needs. His presence accrues incredible interest. Galatians 5:22-23 declares that the fruit of the Spirit yields *"love, joy, peace, patience . . . and self-control,"* available for immediate withdrawal.

Are you spiritually bankrupt? Nothing would delight God more than for you to be "cashing your checks." Seeing yourself through God's eyes, you see that His divine power has given you everything you need for life and godliness. You can bank on it!

Personalize these verses in your own words:

Ephesians 1:3 _____

_____

_____

_____

_____

_____

_____

2 Corinthians 9:8 _____

_____

_____

_____

_____

_____

_____

Father, through Your eyes I can see that I . . . _____

_____

_____

_____

_____

_____

I have worth because . . . I am given everything I need by God.

His Purpose
for Me

"His divine power has given us everything we need for life and godliness through our knowledge of him who called us by his own glory and goodness."
(2 Peter 1:3)

Day 24

I am created to do good works for Christ.

"We are . . . created in Christ Jesus to do good works,
which God prepared in advance for us to do."
(Ephesians 2:10)

We all know what it is like to feel small. As we look around, it is easy to see people performing with peak proficiency—tasks being accomplished with quickness and creativity. In comparison, we often feel small with feelings that we are inadequate, incapable, even inept.

But don't confuse the issue: in God's economy, *bigger isn't always better*. Remember the poor widow in Luke chapter 21 who gave her gift to God? Her "widow's mite" was only one-twentieth of a penny. Based not on the size of her gift, but on the size of her sacrifice, Jesus singled her out saying, *"This poor widow has put in more than all the others"* (Luke 21:3). He was indicating that the small offering from her humble heart had far more value than all the other gifts. The widow's mite was mighty—she had given with a sacrificial heart.

The issue is not size, but sacrifice. The smallest kindness, the smallest deed will not go unnoticed by God. A *small* work is a *great* work when the heart motive is right in God's sight.

> "It is not what a man does that determines whether his
> work is sacred or secular, it is why he does it. The motive is
> everything. Let a man sanctify the Lord God in his heart and
> he can thereafter do no common act."[10] —A. W. Tozer

As a child of God, do you realize that God has already prepared in advance a fulfilling and meaningful work for you to do? This plan was in His mind even before you became His child. Perhaps you might think, *But I'm not really capable of doing anything significant.* Be assured that right now you are fully prepared to do a precious work, a powerful work—a work of love.

I know a woman who takes the "teddy bear stance." All teddy bears have one common characteristic—their arms are always open wide. Think of the people in our world who are never hugged. What a ministry she has encouraging others with a warm embrace! She stands with her arms open wide ready to share God's love.

Have you ever felt insignificant when no one noticed that you were reaching out? Your sacrificial effort may have seemed too small to be appreciated. Remember, as you see yourself through God's eyes, you know that even an unseen deed is not hidden from His view; *"Whatever you did for one of the least of these . . . you did for me"* (Matthew 25:40). No sacrifice of the heart is small in God's sight.

Personalize these verses in your own words:

Psalm 90:17 _____

_____

_____

_____

_____

_____

Colossians 3:23 _____

_____

_____

_____

_____

_____

Father, through Your eyes I can see that I . . . _____

_____

_____

_____

_____

_____

I have value because . . . I am created to do good works for Christ.

Day 25

I am an ambassador for Christ.

"We are . . . Christ's ambassadors."
(2 Corinthians 5:20)

The little girl with blonde curls tapped across the screen into the hearts of millions. Her charm attracted children around the world. Dolls with her name flooded the market. The Texas Rangers made her a captain, while the State of Kentucky made her a colonel. The 165,000 member Kiddies Club of England vowed to "follow faithfully the example she set in character, behavior and personal manners." The phenomenon grew as she starred in film after film.

A reporter once asked, "Shirley Temple, don't you ever get tired of people pushing and shoving, asking questions and demanding your time?" "No, I don't mind at all," she said, "It's part of my job." This was a little girl setting an example, a little girl living to the highest potential of her calling. Child of God, you, too, have a calling. Ephesians 4:1 says, *"Live a life worthy of the calling you have received."* What is your calling? To be an ambassador!

Years later, President Gerald Ford appointed Shirley Temple Black as an ambassador to officially represent the USA to the people of Ghana. What a position of trust! An ambassador is an official messenger of the highest rank sent by one government to another. This resident representative holds sovereign authority from the homeland to represent, speak, minister, influence and negotiate. You, too, have been called to be an ambassador—a representative of Christ to a spiritually starved world in need of the Master's message.

Perhaps you're thinking, *Others might qualify as an ambassador, but not me! I don't have the freedom or the language to be an ambassador—especially in my family or workplace.* Realize that God's power to speak through you is not limited by your lack of freedom. Imprisoned, Paul understood this when he said, *"Pray also for me, that whenever I open my mouth, words may be given me so that I will fearlessly make known the mystery of the gospel, for which I am an ambassador in chains"* (Ephesians 6:19-20).

Because Christ lives in you, His character will be lived through you. You will minister with His mercy. You will represent His righteousness. You will speak with strength. Even when you don't have the freedom to speak, remember that your influence will be conveyed through His Spirit.

Seeing yourself through God's eyes, you are an appointed ambassador—called by the King!

Personalize these verses in your own words:

Ephesians 4:1 _____

_____

_____

_____

_____

_____

_____

Matthew 5:14-16 _____

_____

_____

_____

_____

_____

_____

Father, through Your eyes I can see that I . . . _____

_____

_____

_____

_____

_____

_____

I have value because . . . I am an ambassador for Christ.

Day 26

I am being conformed to Christ.

"For those God foreknew he also predestined
to be conformed to the likeness of his Son."
(Romans 8:29)

Before a thrilled Olympic audience in 1976, Dorothy Hamill created a sensation as she skated to victory with her "Hamill camel." Yet, even more amazing was the fashion sensation she created with "the wedge," later called the "Hamill haircut." In a matter of days, millions of Dorothy Hamill look-alikes took to the ice trying to be duplicates of Dorothy.

Have you ever tried to look like someone else? You bought designer clothes, but they only covered your insecurities. You changed your hairstyle, but that didn't change your self-doubt. How you tried to conform to society's norm!

The word *conformed* can be transitory and changeable, much like Dorothy's hairstyle—*in* one year and *out* the next. However, when God says He predestined you "to be conformed" to Christ, He is not referring to a transitory *outer* change but to a transforming *inner* change. When you are conformed to Christlikeness, you are given the ability to have His character on the inside. This will change your conduct on the outside. You will not be pulled by the popular, pushed by the press or overpowered by politics. Just as Jesus was not controlled by outside pressure, so you are predestined to have that same Christlikeness.

One such man whose character was conformed to Christ's was Olympian Eric Liddell. In 1924, this Scotsman was Great Britain's hope for the 100-meter race. Then the shocking announcement came: the qualifying heat was to be run on a Sunday.

Unthinkable! Eric believed the Sabbath was God's day. He resolved, "I'm not running" . . . not for Scotland, not for Britain, not even for the gold. Though labeled a traitor, he refused to conform to rules that ran against his conscience.

Yet days later, Eric was placed in the 400-meter—a race for which he had not trained. The gun sounded. He was off like a bullet. Flying through the wind, Eric crossed the finish line setting a new world record. From international jeers to cheers, he has been admired for decades as the one who would not conform to the pressures of this world. Why? Because his very life was conformed to the character of Christ. Seeing yourself through God's eyes, you are being conformed to God's plan for you. You will be amazed with His results!

Personalize these verses in your own words.

Hebrews 12:1 _____

_____

_____

_____

_____

_____

_____

Romans 12:2 _____

_____

_____

_____

_____

_____

Father, through Your eyes I can see that I . . . _____

_____

_____

_____

_____

_____

_____

I have value because . . . I am being conformed to Christ.

Day 27

I am complete in Christ.

"You have been made complete."
(Colossians 2:10, NASB)

International fame came in 1919 when his calculations bedazzled the world. He was considered the greatest genius on earth. His theories of relativity revolutionized the scientific community. Highly sought after, he traveled to speak in capitals all over the world. He admitted, however, "It is strange to be known so universally and yet to be so lonely."

These words of Albert Einstein mirror the pain and pathos that have oppressed many human hearts. Loneliness presents a paradox: How can such heaviness come from emptiness? The answer lies in the fact that the heart yearns to be connected with someone significant. God made us that way. However, we have all experienced loneliness: "the state of being cut off from others, a lack of connectedness with another."

The greatest fear of most single people is loneliness. In 1950, one out of every ten households was a single person household (9.5 percent). But in 2000, the number of single person households jumped to one in four (26 percent).[11] Sadly, singles often live under the black cloud of incompleteness. Emotional rain clouds, molded by well-meaning friends, pour out their promises: "One day Mr. Right will come and complete you!" "One day you'll find someone who'll make you whole." No wonder the single is fearful—who wants to be half a person?

Child of God, upon your salvation, you receive the indwelling Christ whose presence produces total fulfillment—complete wholeness. Colossians 2:9-10 assures: *"For in Christ all the fullness of the Deity lives in bodily form, and you have been given fullness in Christ."* To be *full* is "to be at the maximum of, or greatest degree." Nothing more is needed to make you complete.

Three myths need to be blown away: 1) "Singles are always lonely people." No! But they can experience times of isolation. 2) "Singles are not whole people." No! When you have Christ in you, you have the fullness of His deity in you to live through you. 3) "Only singles are lonely." No!

Married individuals can also experience loneliness. But as you see yourself through God's eyes, whether married or single, you can blow away those black clouds of incompleteness and confidently say, "I am one complete person, and one is a *whole* number!"

Personalize these verses in your own words.

John 17:22-23 _____

_____

_____

_____

_____

_____

_____

2 Peter 1:3-4 _____

_____

_____

_____

_____

_____

Father, through Your eyes I can see that I . . . _____

_____

_____

_____

_____

_____

_____

I have value because . . . I am complete in Christ.

Day 28

I am holy before God.

"God did not call us to be impure, but to live a holy life."
(1 Thessalonians 4:7)

Have you ever had difficulty with the Scripture, *"Be holy, because I am holy"* (1 Peter 1:16)? Since most people think being holy is synonymous with being sinless, who could possibly be holy? It's unattainable . . . unimaginable!

One day a friend said to me, "I know *holy* means 'set apart,' but I don't *want* to be set apart. That sounds like having a constant case of measles!" Unfortunately, some people consider the "holy" person as one who lives a monk-like existence, praying 24 hours a day so as not to sin. Holiness, however, does not bring about isolation, but integration—integrating the character of Christ *in* you for His "nature" to be expressed *through* you. Nature? *Nature* simply means "that which is natural."

When I was a little girl, my Uncle Jimmy walked me through his watermelon patch in Idabel, Oklahoma. Holding a tiny black seed he said, "These big melons grew from seeds just like this one." That seemed impossible to me! Yet 80 miles from Idabel is the town of Hope, Arkansas, where something "more impossible" became reality. Young Jason Bright gave his watermelon seed the care and environment to grow . . . naturally. The result? A world record 260-pound watermelon! How? Watermelon seeds simply do what comes naturally to them—they grow. Their seeds are *set apart* by God for that purpose.

When you are set apart by God, holiness is natural. The Father is the gardener; Christ is the seed. With Christ in you, you are set apart to grow to be like Him. First John 3:9 explains, *"No one who is born of God will continue to sin, because God's seed remains in him."* It is natural for the Lord not to sin. Therefore, with God's seed in you, it becomes increasingly natural for *you* not to sin. What seems impossible becomes possible. You are set apart *from sin* and set apart *to God*. You will not become instantly sinless, but you will sin less . . . and less . . . and less.

God calls you holy. As you see yourself through God's eyes and with His presence inside you, He will produce the impossible through you. Why settle for anything less?

Personalize these verses in your own words:

Romans 12:1 _____

_____

_____

_____

_____

_____

_____

2 Corinthians 7:1 _____

_____

_____

_____

_____

_____

_____

Father, through Your eyes I can see that I . . . _____

_____

_____

_____

_____

_____

_____

I have value because . . . I am holy before God.

Day 29

I am clothed with the righteousness of God.

"I put on righteousness as my clothing."
(Job 29:14)

Y ou're at the beach . . . you're famished . . . you find a restaurant . . .
you rush in . . . you spot a sign: "No shirt, no shoes, no service."
The message is clear. To be accepted you must be clothed according to
the restaurant's standard.

God also has a standard. But He makes it possible for you to be
acceptable to Him at all times when He gives you *"righteousness as [your]
clothing."* The word *righteous* in its simplest form means "right" and
"just." The word also means "acquitted, vindicated." Your faith and trust
in Christ enables God to *acquit* you of sin. He doesn't see your sin any
longer, but sees you as clothed with the righteousness of Christ. As such
you are acceptable and properly dressed to "come and dine."

Actually, righteousness has two similar, yet distinct, meanings:
- First, *being* right in God's sight—based on *belief.*
- Second, *doing* right in God's sight—based on *behavior.*

The problem with the second is, *"There is no one righteous, not
even one"* (Romans 3:10). Therefore, if you wanted God's acceptance, it
couldn't be based on all your actions being "right in His sight." God knew
you needed to *"be right"* so that you could learn to *"do right."*

If you have struggled with feeling too unworthy to be called *"the
righteousness of God"* (2 Corinthians 5:21), realize that this "clothing"
you are given is like a uniform that has authority.

Have you ever seen a gigantic 18-wheeler groaning to a stop just
because a police officer walks in front of the traffic and holds up his or
her hand? What gives this person the right to command such respect?
Certainly not parentage, social status, education, personality or even
church affiliation. The officer stands confidently in front of this awesome
"king of the road" because of the *right clothing* . . . the uniform has
undeniable authority.

Did you realize that at the moment of your conversion, you were issued a righteous "uniform"? The Lord not only covered your past, but also gave you authority over your future. With the *"breastplate of righteousness"* (Ephesians 6:14), God gave you power over sin. When you have "righteousness" as your clothing, you are not only acceptable to God, but you also have the authority of God.

As you see yourself through God's eyes, as His child, you have the power that backs the badge.

Personalize these verses in your own words.

2 Corinthians 5:21 _____

_____

_____

_____

_____

_____

Galatians 3:27 _____

_____

_____

_____

_____

Father, through Your eyes I can see that I . . . _____

_____

_____

_____

_____

_____

_____

I have value because . . . I am clothed with
the righteousness of God.

Day 30

I am safe in the protection of God.

*"For you alone, O LORD,
make me dwell in safety."
(Psalm 4:8)*

Tammy, the young trapeze artist, electrified the audience with her daring performance. Afterward, a reporter asked, "How do you appear so confident performing such a dangerous aerial act?" The child quickly broke into a smile and responded, "That's easy. Didn't you see the safety net? There was a man standing there to break my fall. That was my dad."

Nothing frees you to walk the tightrope of life—to perform daring feats outside your comfort zone—like knowing you're safe in your heavenly Father's care. *He holds the net.* In Deuteronomy 33:27 we are promised, *"Underneath are the everlasting arms"* always ready to break our fall.

As a child of God, you face far-reaching challenges . . . trying times when God calls you to unfold your faith under pressure. During these times of severe stress, you can escape trauma and turmoil when you remember . . . *He holds the net.* When your life becomes uneven and your thinking unbalanced, and even though you take a nose dive into the net, your Father breaks the fall . . . *He holds the net.*

When Simon Peter saw Jesus walking on the water, he yearned to step out of the safety of the boat. In a burst of faith he cried out, *"Jesus, let me come to you!"* Throwing caution to the wind, he stepped out onto the water and walked on "his miracle."

Yet only a short time later, Peter would experience a devastating fall: the denial of his Lord . . . not once, not twice, but three times. He had been trusted—he was now a failure.

But no! Peter hadn't seen the unbreakable net of safety, acceptance, and love. Jesus was there with a net full of forgiveness for Peter. Jesus broke the fall.

Where there had been a threefold denial, now Jesus gave Peter the opportunity for a threefold declaration of love: *Peter, do you love Me . . .*

tend My lambs . . . shepherd My sheep . . . feed My sheep. The Lord's gentle coaching prepared Peter for a confident lifetime of ministry.

Do you know the sickening feeling of plummeting to the net? See yourself through God's eyes, and never forget that He stands to break your fall; He ensures your safety. *He holds the net.*

Personalize these verses in your own words:

Psalm 16:1 _____

_____

_____

_____

_____

_____

_____

Romans 8:31 _____

_____

_____

_____

_____

_____

_____

Father, through Your eyes I can see that I . . . _____

_____

_____

_____

_____

_____

_____

I have value because . . . I am safe in the protection of God.

Day 31

I am secure in the love of God.

"I have loved you with an everlasting love."
(Jeremiah 31:3)

"Of all earthly music, that which reaches farthest into heaven is the beating of a truly loving heart."—H.W. Beecher

Who has not longed for love? Who has not sought security, desired devotion, especially commitment from one significant person, only to find yourself empty-handed and empty-hearted? God created each person with an inner need for unconditional love. Yet, we all know what it is like "to have loved and lost."

That is why the love of God is unfathomable. As a child of God, you can never be lost from His love. Nothing you can do will make God love you more. Nothing you can do will make God love you less. He loves you without merit; He loves you without measure.

From 1856 to 1866, when the transatlantic communication cable was being laid, workmen discovered ocean depths they were unable to *fathom*, depths they were unable "to measure or to probe." A weighted line dropped to a depth of 2,000 fathoms (one fathom equals six feet), still did not reach the ocean floor. This depth was called "unfathomable." Similarly, the depth of God's love is beyond measure. *"Can you fathom the mysteries of God? Can you probe the limits of the Almighty?"* (Job 11:7). This is God's love for you!

Perhaps the most poetic expression of God's unfathomable love was written long ago by a man who died in an asylum. These words were found scribbled on the wall beside his bed:

Could we with ink the ocean fill,
And were the skies of parchment made,
Were every stalk on earth a quill,
And every man a scribe by trade.
To write the love of God above
Would drain the ocean dry.

Nor could the scroll contain the whole,
Though stretched from sky to sky.
O, love of God, how rich, how pure!
How measureless and strong!
It shall forevermore endure
The saints' and angels' song.[12]

How can you fathom or understand that God really loves you? In part, by looking at Christ's love for you. His death redeems you; His sacrifice saves you; His life liberates you. In love, He laid down His life for you, so that His life could be lived through you.

Seeing yourself through God's eyes, you can be assured that His love never fails . . . it is forgiving, freeing, fathomless.

Personalize these verses in your own words.

Ephesians 3:17-19 _____

_____

_____

_____

_____

Romans 8:38-39 _____

_____

_____

_____

_____

Father, through Your eyes I can see that I . . . _____

_____

_____

_____

_____

_____

I have value . . . because I am secure in the love of God.

Appendices

God mends the broken heart,
When you give Him all the pieces,
He heals you with His love,
And His care never ceases.
Though you're broken and shattered,
Wounded and scattered,
The pieces don't fit any more.
God mends the broken heart,
Just like it was before.
—June Hunt

HOPE FOR THE HEART
God's Truth for Today's Problems

HOPE FOR THE HEART is a Christ-centered ministry providing Biblically-based counseling material, tapes and CDs on the following topics:

Abortion Prevention
Adoption
Adultery
Aging
Alcohol & Drug Abuse
Anger
Anorexia & Bulimia
Assurance of Salvation
Atheism & Agnosticism
The Bible: Is it Reliable?
The Blended Family
Boundaries
Caregiving
Child Evangelism
Childhood Sexual Abuse
Chronic Illness
Codependency
Communication
Conflict Resolution
Confrontation
Counseling
Critical Spirit
Cults
Dating
Death
Decision Making
Depression
Divorce
Dysfunctional Family
Employment
Envy & Jealousy
Ethics & Integrity
Euthanasia
Evil & Suffering . . . Why?

Fear & Phobias
Financial Freedom
Forgiveness
Friendship
God: Who Is He?
Grief
Guilt
Habits
The Holy Spirit
Homosexuality
Hope
Identity: Who Are You?
Infertility
Intimacy
Islam
Jehovah's Witnesses
Jesus: Is He God?
Jewish Fulfillment
Loneliness
Lying
Manipulation
Marriage
Mentoring
Midlife Crisis
Mormonism
New Age Spirituality
The Occult
Overeating
Parenting
Perfectionism
Pregnancy, Unwanted
Prejudice
Premarital Counseling

Pride & Humility
Procrastination
Prosperity
Purpose in Life
Rape Recovery
Rebellion
Reconciliation
Rejection
Salvation
Satan, Demons & Satanism
Self-Worth
Sexual Addiction
Sexual Temptation
Singleness
Single Parenting
Spiritual Abuse
Spiritual Warfare
Stealing
Stress
Submission
Success through Failure
Suicide Prevention
Teenagers
Temptation
Terminal Illness
Time Management
Trials
Unbelieving Mate
Victimization
Widowhood
Wife Abuse
Workaholism
Worry

P.O. Box 7 • Dallas, TX 75221 • 1-800-488-HOPE (4673) www.hopefortheheart.org

Through years of Biblical study and research, June Hunt has developed practical material on 100 counseling topics, ranging from everyday issues such as forgiveness, fear, grief and guilt to the more damaging issues of anger, abuse, depression and suicide. Her ministry at HOPE FOR THE HEART responds with help, healing and hope for those in the midst of the struggle.

You can hear June on the *HOPE FOR THE HEART* daily radio broadcast and on *HOPE IN THE NIGHT*, her two-hour, live call-in program. For a broadcast schedule of stations and times, call **1-800-488-HOPE (4673)**.

To receive a free catalog of Scripturally-based counseling helps, please contact:

HOPE FOR THE HEART
P.O. Box 7
Dallas, Texas 75221

Or call
1-800-488-HOPE (4673)
www.hopefortheheart.org

HOPE
for the Heart

*"For I know the plans I have for you . . .
plans to give you hope and a future."
(Jeremiah 29:11)*

HOPE FOR THE HEART wants to help you in your personal quest for spiritual growth and healing. If you have grown personally as a result of this material and would like to receive additional resources from the ministry of HOPE FOR THE HEART, please fill out the coupon below and send it to us. Or call our toll-free product number, 1-800-488-HOPE (4673) or visit our website: www.hopefortheheart.org

---

Yes!

I would like to receive additional information and materials from HOPE FOR THE HEART.

Name _____

Address _____

City _____

State _____ Zip _____

E-mail address _____

Mail to:

HOPE FOR THE HEART
P. O. Box 7
Dallas, TX 75221
www.hopefortheheart.org

Endnotes

1. Charles H. Spurgeon, *Morning and Evening: Daily Readings* (Lynchburg, VA: The Old-Time Gospel Hour, n.d.), 111.

2. Anna B. Warner and David Rutherford McQuire, "Jesus Loves Me" (n.p.: n.p., 1860).

3. E. Y. Harburg, "Over the Rainbow" (n.p.: n.p., 1938).

4. Corrie ten Boom, John L. Sherrill, and Elizabeth Sherrill, *The Hiding Place* (Washington Depot, CT: Chosen, 1971), 192-3.

5. William Orcutt Cushing, "Under His Wings" (n.p.: n.p., n.d.).

6. Larry Richards, *Expository Dictionary of Bible Words*, Regency Reference Library, electronic ed. (Grand Rapids: Zondervan, 1985).

7. James L. Nicholson, "Whiter Than Snow," in *Joyful Songs* No. 4 (Philadelphia, PA: Methodist Episcopal Book Room, 1872), n.p.

8. William J. Kirkpatrick, "Lord I'm Coming Home," in *Winning Songs* (Philadelphia, PA: John J. Hood, 1892), n.p.

9. Annie J. Flint, "He Giveth More Grace," Casterline Card Series, no. 5510 (Oxford Park, NY: n.p., n.d.).

10. A. W. Tozer, *The Pursuit of God*, Tozer Legacy ed. (Camp Hill, PA: Christian, 1993), 127.

11. Frank Hobbs and Nicole Stoops, U. S. Census Bureau, *Demographic Trends in the 20th Century*, Census 2000 Special Reports, Series CENSR-4 (Washington, DC: U. S. Government Printing Office, 2002), 2.

12. Frederick M. Lehman, "The Love of God," in *Songs That Are Different*, vol. 2 (n.p.: n.p., 1919), n.p.

Here's more help in continuing your spiritual journey! Join June on her website.

Find the latest news and information.

www.hopefortheheart.org

Seeing Yourself Through God's Eyes
Leader's Guide

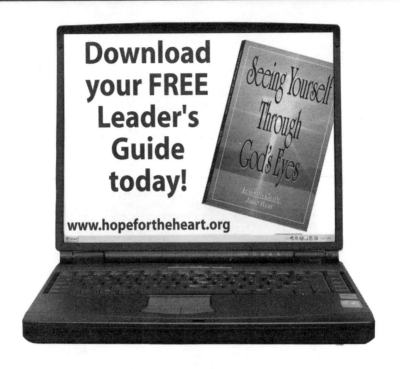

The Leader's Guide offers:

- Step-by-step encouragement in journaling each section

- Helpful tips for group interaction

- More Biblical references for answering questions about self-worth

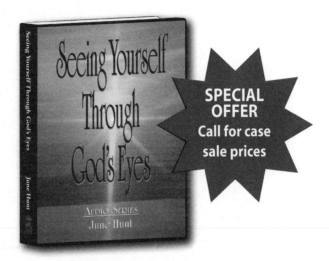